LORRIES ILLUSTRATED
ATKINSON

Peter Davies

Roundoak Publishing

First published in 2000 by
Roundoak Publishing
The Old Dairy, Perry Farm,
East Nynehead, Wellington,
Somerset TA21 ODA

Tel. 01823 461997 Fax 01823 461998
email: info@nynehead-books.co.uk
website: nynehead-books.co.uk

ISBN 1 871565 35 9

Design by Peter Davies

Origination by Roundoak Associates

Printed in Great Britain by
The Amadeus Press, Huddersfield

Left: Though not part of Atkinson's standard
range this Chinese Six artic is the stuff that
stops enthusiasts in their tracks. Using a 1973
'Borderer' as a basis, John Killingbeck of
Blackburn, Lancashire, created this stunning
machine by adding a second steering axle.
The conversion was carried out in 1986.
Killingbeck's, which closed down at the
beginning of 1999, ran one of the country's
most memorable Atkinson fleets.

ATKINSON

A pictorial record of Atkinsons at work from the early 'Sixties to the mid 'Eighties

The author pictured with his preserved
Atkinson Borderer back in 1986

Atkinsons have a special place in
the memories of lorry enthusiasts.
It is now a quarter of a century
since the last ones were built at the
famous Walton-le-Dale factory.
This book looks back at some of the best
known Atkinsons, captured on film during
their working days. It not only brings the
lorries to life but depicts them in their
authentic period liveries, many of which
have faded into history.
All the colour shots were taken by the
author over a period of some 25 years.
Together they form a unique record of a
past era in British road haulage. An era
when Britain was a major player in the
truck manufacturing world.
Why not sit back and enjoy this trip
down memory lane.

Peter Davies February 2000

Contents

KNIGHTS OF THE ROAD

Atkinson epitomises the British commercial vehicle at its best during the late '30s and the post war years when British-built lorries were among the finest in the world. Small wonder that so many enthusiasts nowadays look upon them as great classics. In their day they were the undisputed 'knights of the road' and the Knight's Head motif so proudly displayed on their radiators symbolised British craftsmanship at its best.

It was in 1907 that Edward Atkinson and his brother Harry, together with a partner George Hunt, set up an engineering business, Atkinson & Co. at Frenchwood Avenue, Preston. The company soon moved to bigger premises at Kendal Street, undertaking motor and steam wagon repairs. It took on a repair agency for Alley & MacLellan, manufacturers of the famous Sentinel Steam Waggon, built at that time in Polmadie, Glasgow. By 1916 Edward Atkinson had decided to build a wagon of his own design, having relinquished the Alley & MacLellan agency when Sentinel moved to Shrewsbury in 1915.

Demand for road transport had grown rapidly following the outbreak of World War 1 and the horse and cart was giving way to self-propelled vehicles, so Atkinson's first steam wagon of 1916 found plenty of customers. It is no coincidence that the Atkinson '6T' (6-tonner) bore some

likeness to the Sentinel 'Standard' since Edward Atkinson employed Joe Haythorne, an ex-Alley & MacLellan draughtsman, to do the design work. Chassis no. 1 was completed in 1916 and was later registered CK490. It was based on a 10ft. 6in. wheelbase and weighed 7½ tons fully fuelled up with

coal, water and oil.

Like Alley & MacLellan's Sentinel, the Atkinson featured a vertical water-tube boiler. An easily removable superheater coil was fitted and the boiler working pressure was 200 psi. Exhaust steam was used to pre-heat the feed water. The double-acting

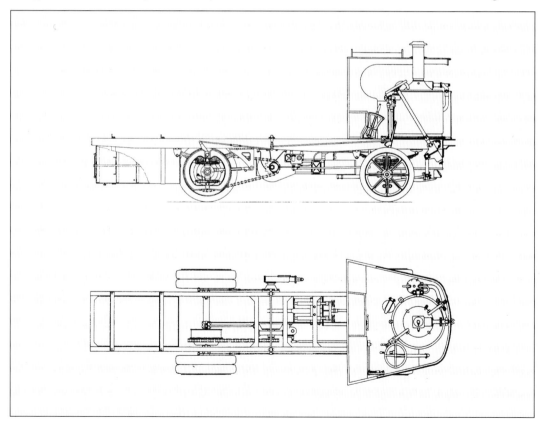

Above: Supplied in 1923, this 6-ton wagon was operated by Shephard & Hough, haulage contractors of Stirchley, Birmingham. It ran on contract to Worthington's Brewery.

Left: General arrangement drawing of the Atkinson 6-ton 'Uniflow' steam lorry of 1924. In side profile it bore some resemblance to the Sentinel 'Standard'.

2-cylinder 'Duplex' engine had a bore and stroke of 6.75in. x 10in. and ran at 300 rpm. It featured patented ball type inlet and exhaust valves.

The camshaft provided two forward cut offs at 50% and 70% plus one reverse at 75%. A fully open position was also provided for blow-through during warm up. Drive to the rear axle was by a single chain, driven from a sprocket mounted on to the offside end of the crankshaft, and a differential was incorporated into the rear axle next to the drive sprocket.

Steam wagon production survived

up to 1929, the highest chassis number being '547' but it is not certain that this represents the real production total, which may have been lower. There were some significant design changes during the thirteen years of production. Quite early on, in 1919, a new engine of the American-designed double-acting 'Uniflow' type was introduced with a bore and stroke of 7in. x 10in. The Uniflow engine was standard by 1920. A smaller 2½-ton wagon was built in 1921 but, apparently, this did not enter series production.

Despite producing successful steam wagons, Atkinson was in financial difficulties following the post war slump of the '20s. A brief but unsuccessful merger with Walker Bros of Wigan in 1925, under which the products were called Atkinson-Walker wagons, ended in 1930. With no prospect of recovery the company fell into the hands of the receivers who eventually sold it to St Helens based speculators J. Jenkins, H. Johnson and J. Lytheer in 1931. At first the rescued company carried on with steam wagon repairs as well as carrying out third-axle conversions and the building of drawbar trailers but two or three experimental diesel lorries were also built during 1931-32.

One was a 6-ton four wheeler, the other a 12-ton six wheeler dubbed the 'A1'. These were powered by 6-cylinder Blackstone 'BMV6' diesel engines with auxiliary petrol-powered starting engines. A remote 4-speed gearbox was fitted. A bonneted four wheeler with Dorman diesel engine was also tried. This was powered by a '4RBL' and the drive was taken through a Meadows 4-speed gearbox to a Moss worm-drive rear axle. All these machines pre-dated the true Atkinson lorries which were introduced after 1933.

Following the death of Edward Atkinson in 1932, a London businessman, W. G. Allen of Nightingale's Garage, bought the business and it was renamed Atkinson Lorries (1933) Ltd. It was then decided to build diesel-engined lorries to compete with the likes of Foden and ERF. They featured Gardner diesels, David Brown gearboxes, Kirkstall axles and vacuum hydraulic brakes.

Full production got underway in 1935 when the company moved to larger premises in Marsh Lane and in the four years up to the beginning of World War 2 some fifty lorries were built. These included four, six and eight wheelers as well as twin steer six wheelers. The very first models bore some resemblance to their ERF contemporaries. Where ERFs had two parallel diagonal lines across their radiators the early Atkinsons had two horizontal lines (the circle 'A' badge was added in 1937). Mechanically the two makes also had a lot in common. Over the years they developed along similar lines although ERF became more adventurous in their cab styling while Atkinson retained their traditional 'outside rad' throughout most of their existence.

Atkinson was one of the few UK manufacturers allowed to continue civilian truck production during the

Top: This bonneted machine was the first Atkinson diesel lorry and was completed in 1932. Power came from a Dorman 4RBL. It had manual brakes which were later converted to vacuum servo.

Above: This rare vehicle is believed to be the second Atkinson and was basically a forward control version of the first. It was built to the order of the Italian Ministry of War in 1932.

war, under the direction of the government. From 1939 to 1942 production concentrated on six wheelers but from then on it switched to eight wheelers. Wartime shortages of Gardner engines led to the use of AEC 7.7 litre diesels. Three out of every four wartime Atkinsons were AEC powered. In the post war years Gardners were reinstated as the standard power units but AEC engines continued to be available to customers' special order.

Atkinson model designations were easy to understand as they were made up of the payload rating, number of wheels and the number of cylinders. For example, '745' meant a 7-ton four wheeler with 5-cylinder engine. The figures were prefixed by 'L', 'M' or 'S' indicating long, medium or short

Above: An early Atkinson press advertisement.

wheelbase. Tractor units were given a 'T' prefix while twin-steer lorries were prefixed 'TS'. A 'T' suffix indicated a tipper chassis. Later on, during the '60s, the payload figure was replaced by a gross weight figure - e.g. the 'L1786' eight wheeler (17-ton payload) became an 'L2486' (24 tons gvw). As the trusty old Gardner LW range was joined by alternative power units, model designations had another suffix added. For instance, an 'X' indicated a Gardner 6LX '150' and 'XB' meant 6LXB '180'. Likewise other makes of engine were identified by a letter -'C' for Cummins, 'RR' for Rolls Royce, etc. In the 'sixties the suffix 'A' was also used to denote air brakes.

Post war demand was such that Atkinson moved into a new, larger, factory at Winery Lane, Walton le Dale in 1947. The Marsh Lane site survived as a service centre until 1957. It was, by then, one of the UK's leading truck builders and it had built up a healthy export trade. Throughout the '50s and '60s Atkinson went on to produce a huge variety of road going and specialised trucks. While its mainstream products were forward control load carriers it diversified, from the late '50s, into heavy duty dumptrucks, heavy haulage and special oilfield tractors like the massive bonneted 'Omega' of 1957. That was powered by a 333 bhp supercharged Rolls Royce C6.SFL coupled to a Self Changing Gears eight-speed semi-automatic gearbox and was capable of hauling 90 tons over desert terrain.

As Atkinson's world markets expanded assembly plants were established - in Australia in 1962 and, in 1968, South Africa and New Zealand where vehicles were tailored to local operating conditions. These resulted in comparatively rare breeds of Atkinsons with their own cabs, engines and transmissions, completely

Left: As Atkinson Lorries (1933) Ltd the company began building the more familiar looking forward control range although the 'Circle A' badge did not appear until 1937. This is an early Gardner 4LW-powered 6/7-tonner with vacuum hydraulic brakes.

7
7

Left: By 1938 when this magnificent L1586 rigid eight wheeler was built Atkinsons had taken on their distinctive appearance which was to remain almost unchanged through to the early fifties.

and an elaborate full width grille. It had set forward doors hinged at the 'A' pillar and a single piece windscreen. Once again, no one seemed impressed. The prototype, which was displayed at Earls Court in 1964, was destined for Bulwark Transport to undergo appraisal. There are no records of other Guardsmans except for one reported as being available in the show's Demonstration Park.

Atkinson's next bold attempt at modernisation was the slightly more successful 'View Line' announced in 1966. If anything, it was ahead of its time and would not have looked out of place in the '90s. It stood 9ft 10in tall and had a massive windscreen, approximately 36in deep. The very first View Line had a flashy full-width slatted grille but production models, once again in response to customer preference, had the exposed radiator, albeit a fibreglass dummy.

Atkinson seemed to abandon any further plans to modernise and settled for a slightly enlarged version of the existing fibreglass cab which was dubbed the Mk.2. This had an improved driving position and slightly better interior trim but, compared with the competition when it appeared in 1968, it was still old fashioned. In spite of this the Mk.2 was to live on until Atkinson production ended in 1975.

different from UK-sourced vehicles. From the late 1950s Atkinson fitted fibreglass cabs for the UK market while overseas customers generally preferred steel cabs which were often locally built.

During the 1960s Atkinson made several attempts to update its cabs to get away from the old fashioned 'outside rad' style. Curiously, all such attempts were unsuccessful. It seems that customers in general liked the solid, traditional look. The first facelift came in the form of the 'Bodyline' with its full width grille and concealed radiator. It was announced in 1963 as a variation on the Mk.1 fibreglass cab. It didn't appeal to many customers but one feature, the four headlamp system, was adopted for the standard Mk.1, which retained the aluminium exposed radiator.

The T3048C 'Guardsman' of 1964 was an even bigger departure. The Cummins V8E-235 engined Guardsman featured radical new ideas

As well as the many variations on its haulage range cabs, Atkinson built quite a number of bonneted cabs like the 'SBT' (semi-bonneted tractor) for Pickfords and the 'BT' (bonneted tractor) for heavy haulage use. Then there were the 'half cabs' which went on its range of Hy-lode dumptrucks.

In 1968 Atkinson tried to increase its share of the European market by fitting Krupp steel tilt cabs when Krupp of Essen in Germany sold out to Daimler-Benz and phased out truck production. Atkinson Vehicles (Europe) was set up in Antwerp, Belgium but the venture was short-lived. Most Krupp-cabbed Atkis were basically 'Silver Knight' models powered by Rolls Royce engines but they also featured revised front suspension to give a softer ride.

The company was renamed Atkinson Vehicles Ltd from 1954 and, in 1970, was the subject of a take-over by Seddon Diesel Vehicles Ltd of Oldham. Thus Seddon-Atkinson Vehicles was born. The last Atkinson badged vehicles were built just five years later. Seddon-Atkinson's independence was itself short lived - the company was taken over by International Harvester of North America in 1974. International was seeking to strengthen its presence in Europe and already had a 33% holding in DAF Trucks of Eindhoven, Holland. The last hint of Atkinson's identity is the presence of their distinctive 'circle A' badge which, by popular demand, was re-introduced on Seddon-Atkinson vehicles in 1982 and still survives today within the Iveco group.

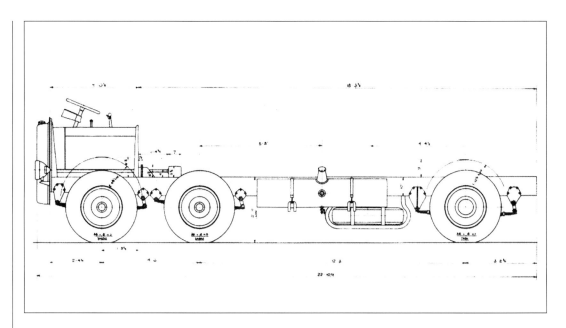

Above: In common with Foden and Leyland, Atkinson were quick to introduce a 9/10-ton payload twin-steer, a type pioneered by ERF. This drawing shows the layout of the late 'thirties version. It was basically the front end of an eight wheeler matched to the rear end of a four wheeler.

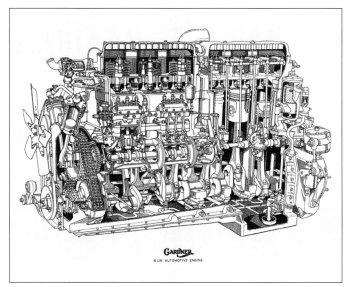

GARDNER
6 LW AUTOMOTIVE ENGINE

Left: The leading power unit for most Atkinson heavies up to the late 'fifties was the legendary Gardner 6LW 112bhp 6-cylinder oil engine.

VARIATIONS ON THE BIG 'A'

Over a period of forty years or so Atkinson built an astonishing variety of types - even a few 'one-offs'. Some of their specialised models have been brought together in this pictorial round-up.

Top row, left to right:
Underfloor-engined 1953 L744HL with Gardner 4HLW and three-seater cab.

Export 6x4 tractors were for various gross weights up to 150 tons.

Semi-forward 32-ton 'SBT' 6x2 tractor in Pickfords Tank Haulage fleet.

Atkinson's first 'Viewline' seen here in Hall's of Sidcup livery.

The massive 'Omega' tractor could haul 90 tons across desert terrain.

Middle row, left to right:
A prototype underfloor-engined lorry for Carlsberg lager.

DMT of Lincoln ran this one-off artic with Ruston air-cooled diesel.

Ultra short eight wheel tipper with Taylor-Hull cab in New Zealand.

Later 'Viewlines' had the traditional 'exposed' radiator re-instated.

A special 150-ton hot ingot carrier for Stewarts & Lloyds steelworks.

Bottom row, left to right:
Australian four wheeled tipper with bespoke pattern steel cab.

Australian-built Atkinsons were tailored to local conditions.

This Bulwark 'Guardsman' was a virtual one-off which appeared in 1964.

One of a range of heavy duty dumpers which appeared during the 'sixties.

Motorway snowplough-gritter built for the Ministry of Transport.

11

FLASHBACK TO THE '64 SHOW

In 1964 Atkinson Vehicles Ltd was enjoying healthy sales and its product range was second to none. Many leading companies were placing repeat orders and Atkinson's Earls Court Show stand was a clear reflection of their success. Legendary names like Suttons, Pickfords, Bulwark, Hansons, Reeds and Peter McCallum spoke volumes for Atkinson's reputation. In that era manufacturers proudly showed off the famous liveries of their leading customers and a visit to Earls Court was an enjoyable and rewarding experience. This aerial view of the 1964 show recalls one of Atkinson's most memorable displays.

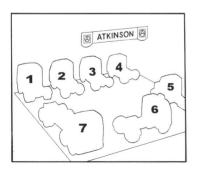

Left: keyline guide to the Atkinson stand at the 1964 Earls Court Show. Vehicles on display were:

1. Cummins V8-powered T3048C with 'FE' Guardsman cab for Bulwark Transport.

2. Cummins NH220-powered T3046C with Mk.1 cab for Peter McCallum.

3. A typical T746XA tractor unit with Mk.1 fibreglass cab and Gardner 6LX.

4. A Gardner 5LW-engined 'Weightmaster' WT45A tractor unit for Reed Transport.

5. This semi-forward SBT3266X tractor unit was destined for Pickfords.

6. Sutton and Son were the owners of this T2846X with Gardner 6LX '150'.

7. A classic 'Mk.1' rigid eight S1786XLA tipper chassis supplied to R. Hanson.

The Past in Colour
Atkinsons through the lens

Part 1 : 'Bow Fronts' 1952 to 1964

Left: If one were asked to describe the archetypal British eight wheeler of the 'fifties this 1958 L1786 of A.M. Walker would be worth a thousand words. Walker's fleet of 35 wagons was built up after 1954 mainly with ex-BRS Atkinsons. Miss A.M. Walker, the chairwoman, was formerly boss of Kinders Transport of Blaby. Walker's memorable fleet of Atkis was mainly engaged on long distance traffic to South Wales, the North West and North East carrying steel, bricks and concrete products.

Right: One of the best known fleets in the UK is that of Marley Tiles with headquarters at Riverhead, Sevenoaks in Kent. This Gardner '150' engined eight wheeler dates from 1960 and features the wider radiator usually indicative of the higher powered Gardners (not that they really needed extra cooling - they tended to take hours to warm up!) The shot was taken on the outskirts of Edinburgh.

Left: A 1953 L1586 of Seaguard Marine Coatings parked up in the sunshine at Swansea in South Wales. Shod on 40x8 tyres, this is an archetypal example of a British eight wheeler of the 'fifties. It has all the 'classic' features of a Gardner 6LW, David Brown gearbox, Kirkstall rear axles and a 24ft flat body with mid-height loading board.

Right: Even in 1965 when this L2486 4000-gallon fuel tanker was registered, the 'bow-front' cab was still available. The vehicle was part of the Alfred Manchester fleet from Anchor & Hope Lane, Charlton in East London. Typical of Gardner-powered tankers of its era, it is equipped with a transverse front exhaust, to petroleum regulations, mounted so that it discharges to the nearside.

Left: 420GRE is a particularly rare beast - it was one of a handful of L1588 rigid eight wheelers built around 1955 with the 150bhp 8LW 'straight eight' Gardner. It was new to Craddock Bros of Coven, Wolverhampton and is seen here later in life after being sold on to Bob Wilson's well known amusement company of Redditch and Leysdown-on-Sea. It was photographed at Ealing Common Fair in August 1970.

Right: A scene which could not be repeated in this day and age is this shot of a 1956 L1586 tanker of C.E. Dormer Ltd of Leyton in East London making its way along the A6 trunk road through the heart of Luton. That route was de-trunked in the 'sixties after the M1 was opened and George Street, the backdrop to this shot, has long since been transformed into a pedestrian precinct.

Left: A T746 artic of Alfred Dexter Ltd of London and Liverpool, grinds its way slowly up Archway Road on a summer's evening in 1966. Highgate Archway can be seen in the background and the relatively quiet conditions are an evocative reminder of the 'sixties. Dexter's were mainly fruit hauliers regularly loading out of the old Covent Garden fruit market and making nightly runs to Liverpool.

Right: This Duramin-cabbed Atkinson L1786 tanker was part of the John Ancliff fleet based at Urmston, Trafford Park. Ancliff was a sub division of the large Bulwark Transport organisation based at Chippenham. This explains the Wiltshire registration number 'RMW'. Ancliff's specialised in all kinds of bulk liquid transport and later, as part of Bulwark, merged into United Transport.

21

Left: The old established Aaron Henshall company of Hope Street, Prescot near Liverpool had a fine fleet of Atkinsons, many of which were six wheelers, often seen hauling drawbar trailers. This L1266 is a typical example dating from 1955. Henshall became part of the well known Holt Lane Transport fleet in the 'seventies, also based at Prescot.

Right: The celebrated fleet of Sutton & Son was predominantly Atkinson during the 'sixties. As well as their long distance six and eight wheeled flats, the company ran a number of chemical tankers including this 1954 S745 based on a tipper wheelbase. It is seen at Sutton's main depot and headquarters in St Helens, Lancashire.

Above: 'Chinese Sixes' were far less common than eight leggers. This machine, officially designated a TS1065, was new to H. Tabern of St Helens and was later operated by J. Barrett of Delph near Oldham. When it was retired from duty in the 'seventies it was preserved. During its working life it carried general goods varying from cotton bales to farm implements.

Right: If one were asked to find a British lorry embodying all the classic ingredients, one would need to look no further than this 1958 'bow-front' L1786 from the fleet of J. Williamson Ltd of Bishopton Road, Stockton-on-Tees. Williamson's fleet of fifteen wagons ran regular services between Tees-side, Lancashire and London.

Left: Though dating from 1962 this L1786 of the Parkfield Garage & Transport Company, Wolverhampton, hardly differs from its counterparts of the early 'fifties. The lorry was photographed about to unload a couple of large steel coils at a motor factory in Bedfordshire.

Right: Gateshead is the setting for this shot of a 1962 L1786 'bow-front' from the well known McPhee's fleet based at City Road, Newcastle on Tyne. Although the Mk.1 fibreglass cabs with wrap-round screens had been introduced in 1958, the coachbuilt 'bow-fronts' were still available well into the 'sixties. 10STN would have been powered by a 150bhp Gardner '6LX' oil engine.

Left: Originally registered in 1945, JVT91 began life as a six wheeler and was later converted to a rigid eight by the addition of a second steer. It was also re-cabbed with a 'bow-front' cab during the late 'fifties. This veteran of the Sutton & Son fleet is seen being unloaded at the company's London depot in 1969.

Right: Toiling up Barnet Hill in North London late on a July evening in 1968 is this re-cabbed, 1944 registered, rigid eight 'L1586' loaded high with glass containers. It was part of the celebrated Sutton & Son long distance fleet which regularly operated between the company's home base at St Helens and its London depot at St Clement Street.

29

Left: Aylesbury-based Goss Transport Ltd operated this 1957 eight wheeled flat seen here in April 1968 outside a printing works in Crescent Road, Luton, waiting to unload. Note the optional chrome front bumper bar, an unusual feature in the bow-front era.

Right: BRS was a large user of Atkinson eight wheelers during the 'fifties and this classic example, a 1952 L1586 from Chesterfield Branch, was photographed heading north along Regent Road, Bootle in August 1966.

Above: Seen here in the livery of GLS Transport of High Road, Whetstone in North London, this 1961 eight wheeled oil tanker started life as Fleet No.439 in the large Bulwark Transport fleet from Chippenham in Wiltshire. Though dating from the 'bow-front' era, YAM392 has a bespoke cab by Kenning Coachworks Ltd.

Part 2 : Mk.1 Models 1958 to 1969

Left: This 1969 L1646 flat worked in the David Cowell fleet of Prescot near Liverpool mainly carrying goods for the BICC cable works. It began life with a large Yorkshire brewery. The beautifully turned out four wheeler wears Cowell's traditional style red and maroon livery.

Right: W.H. Bowker of Blackburn operated a large Atkinson fleet during the 'sixties and KBV759E is a fine example of their long distance vehicles. The 1967 T3046XB is seen here coupled to a 12 metre tilt semi-trailer used on European traffic. After being retired from active service the tractor unit was preserved by the company. It was one of the first Atkinson tractor units to be built with the Gardner 6LXB '180'.

Left: Dating from 1964 this fully laden L1786X eight wheeled bulk tipper had just pulled off the weighbridge at a large feed mill in Liverpool docks. It was part of the Roberts Transport fleet of Knighton, Radnorshire. The picture dates from 1971.

Right: Engaged on similar traffic to the Gibbs vehicle on page 43, this superb 1967 rigid eight wheeled L2486C is from the smart fleet of T & M Catto of Bucksburn, Aberdeen. Like the Gibbs motor it has a demountable fridge box. It was photographed in north London, some 500 miles from base.

Left: Photographed at Henlow, Bedfordshire in 1970 this T2846 is depicted during the transition of the well known Tyburn Road Tank Co. into a new guise as part of Powell Duffryn's Stephenson Clarke operations. The tank semi-trailer is in the new livery while the tractor, Fleet No.313, still wears the old Tyburn maroon. The company was taken over by Powell Duffryn in 1962 but kept its own livery, including the distinctive 'Tyburn Keeps Good Time' logo (carried over from its forerunner, H.Viney of Preston) until 1970.

Right: One of Craddock Bros. of Coven's Mk.1 eight wheeled flats heads into London along the East India Dock Road on a sunny afternoon in September 1970. EBF488 dates from 1962 and wears Craddock's magnificent traditional green and red livery, once a familiar sight, especially up and down the A5 trunk road.

Left: This 1969 TRS3266XB 5-axle tank outfit makes an impressive sight as it negotiates a roundabout on the outskirts of Brownhills in Staffordshire. The vehicle belonged to the large A.S. Jones fleet from Liverpool which eventually became part of P & O Roadtanks. Five axle artics became common in the 1965 to 1969 period when maximum weight 32-tonners were not practical on four axles owing to outer axle spread regulations.

Right: One of Scotland's finest. Before the days of 38 ton artics with 13.6m fridge trailers, hauliers from around Aberdeen and Fraserburgh used eight wheeled flats with demountable 24ft refrigerated containers. One would have to go a long way to find a finer example than this 1962 Gibbs of Fraserburgh L1786X, 'The Northern Lights', seen here with its Gardner 6LX gently ticking over whilst warming up one morning at Perth in 1970.

Left: Sutton & Son of St Helens ran this 1968 TRS3266 'Silver Knight' on contract to ICI Chemicals. The tank semi-trailer carries a TIR plate indicating that it was engaged on European traffic. Five-axle 32 ton gcw outfits like this one diminished in numbers after more liberal UK legislation was introduced in 1968.

Right: A 1968 L2686XB 'Black Knight' rigid eight with 30ft flat operated by civil engineering contractor A. Monk of Warrington. One problem with these pre-1972 heavy duty eight wheelers was their poor turning circle resulting from an exceptionally long outer axle spread required by law to qualify for the increased gvw.

Left: Dee Valley Transport of Regent Street, Llangollen were the proud owners of this 1966 T2846X artic. The company founder, Jack Edwards, sold out to Pearsons (Hauliers) Ltd of Liverpool in the mid 'sixties but the distinctive red livery was retained and Dee Valley survived until 1994. Before the take-over by Pearsons, DVT's lorries carried evocative fleet names like 'Pride of the Vale', 'Queen of the Valley' and 'Lily of the Valley'.

Right: Load carrying tractor units hauling semi-trailers, known as 'dromedary' outfits, are very rare in the UK. One of the few firms to have run them was J. Spurling Ltd of West Ferry Road, Millwall in East London. This Cummins-engined TS3266C Chinese Six five-axle outfit with Boden semi-trailer features three spherical Interconsult tanks each capable of taking 7 tons of bulk salt.

Left: Registered in 1960, this L1786X flat with load of sawn timber was operated by Shorthouse Bros of Wolverhampton. It was 17 years old and had put in quite a few years' hard graft by the time this shot was taken in 1977.

Right: Taken at Sutton & Sons' Sutton Heath headquarters, this mouth-watering array of Mk.1s would surely raise the pulse of any Atki enthusiast! Centrepiece is fleet no.462, UDJ383, with about as perfect a sheeted load as one could wish for. This was a typical scene at Sutton's huge 17-acre site when this shot was taken in 1967.

Left: Liverpool Docks is the setting for this shot of a nicely turned out L1786X bulk feed carrier belonging to the well known Preston Farmers group. It dates from 1960 and is a first class example of its type. Bulk transport had only come into its own during the 'fifties.

Right: Rigid eight wheeled concrete mixers were not that common but this is one of a fleet of such vehicles once owned by Trumix, part of the Lime-Sand Mortar group. It is based on a 1964 S1786X tipper chassis and was captured on film leaving a site at Leeds in South Yorks back in 1969. The trucks had Gardner 150s, 10-speed David Brown gearboxes and eight-wheeled braking. The 9 cu.yd mixers were supplied by Stothert & Pitt Ltd of Bath.

Left: During the 'fifties and early 'sixties Hague Transport of Ormskirk boasted one of the grandest traditional style liveries of two-tone red, blue and gold but in the mid 'sixties the company adopted this modern paint job in plain blue. This Mk.1 cabbed artic dates from 1964 and was pictured at Hague's yard.

Right: Having 'tipped' its load of sheet steel, Pollock's magnificent 1963 L1786X 'Night Scotsman' weighs out at Vauxhall Motors H-Block steel stores in Luton on the 16th June 1969. Next job will be to drag the rolled up sheets down on to the flat and rope them on before setting out to find a backload for the long journey back to Musselburgh.

54

Left: When it comes to transport liveries, Pollock of Musselburgh have few equals and when the splendour of their livery is matched to an Atki eight legger the result is pretty awesome. HSF10E, Pollock's fleet No.27, bearing the fleet name 'Concord', was photographed in the evening sunshine, parked up for the night just off the Great North Road at Grantham, Lincs in June 1967.

Right: The old Packhorse Café on the A5 near Markyate is the location of this almost new T3046X of Jeune & Hayman of Peckham. J & H had a depot and changeover point here and this 1965 registered artic was photographed in its first year of operation. It is coupled to a York 33ft tandem.

Right: Anyone with an eye for a 'nice wagon' could not fail to be impressed with this fully laden 6-axle drawbar outfit of Holt Lane Transport of Whiston, Prescot. The L1786X dates from 1960 and wears the famous BICC (British Insulated Callender's Cables) contract livery, while the drawbar trailer is in Holt Lane's standard blue and red. The incurable lorry fanatic could study this 'jewel in the crown' of British lorries for hours. It has everything the connoisseur looks for - the gentle film of road dirt, the random mix of wheel centres (40x8s of course!), a traditional 24ft flat with mid-height loading board, one windscreen wiper, seagull rear wings and autolube. Enjoy it - you'll never see the likes of it again.

Left: This 1962 T746X, No.474 in the Sutton & Son fleet, is seen with a return load of 60 fold down stillages normally used to transport car windscreens. The semi-trailer is a York 30ft flat. Sutton's boasted one of the largest and finest Atkinson fleets in the 'sixties with over a hundred examples of the marque, including artics and four, six and eight wheel rigids operating from its St Helens headquarters.

Right: CGM624C, from the fleet of D M Smith of Wishaw, Lanarkshire is a relatively rare Black Knight four wheeler. D M Smith was one of the best known Scottish hauliers, with a traditionally liveried fleet of long distance lorries which were seen throughout the UK.

Left: J.W. Green's old brewery in the heart of Luton forms the backdrop to this 1960 Atkinson L1786 tanker of Whitbread's. Many of Whitbread's Atkinsons had AEC 11.3 diesels. Whitbread took over Green's, who owned the Flowers brand, in the 'sixties. Their tankers made regular deliveries direct to the Continent via the Tilbury to Antwerp roll-on roll-off ferry.

Right: Perfection is Atki-shaped. Some wagons exude character and enthusiast-appeal. That being so, 343TTB would be guaranteed to stop all Atkinson enthusiasts in their tracks. This maximum capacity 32 ton outfit consisting of a 1961 L1786X and Carrimore 18ft drawbar trailer was a real stunner from the fleet of Athersmith Brothers of Abbey Road Garage, Barrow-in-Furness. The company was absorbed into T. Brady & Sons Ltd, also of Barrow, in the early 'seventies. Brady's themselves closed down in 1999.

Above: The Chapman Group, which absorbed J.G. Fielder of Bradford in the 'sixties, were the owners of this 1961 L1786X photographed at the firm's Bradford yard in October 1969. An interesting point to note is the fitment of 900x20 tyres on the front and 40x8s on the rear, a practice followed by some long distance hauliers to achieve a slight speed increase and improved brake cooling.

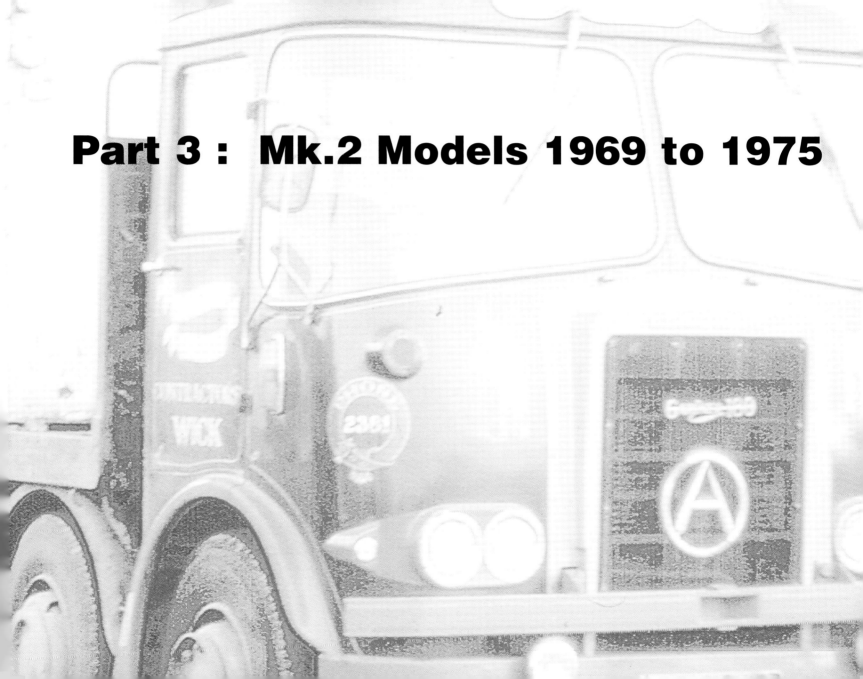

Part 3 : Mk.2 Models 1969 to 1975

Left: An early Mk.2 cabbed eight wheel flat, YAY66J, seen in the famous colours of Ernest Thorpe of Thurgoland, near Sheffield. Thorpe's Atkinsons were instantly recognisable by their white bull-bars and most carried fleet names, in this case 'Sez-Lez'. This is the early version of the Mk.2 fibreglass cab with the wiper pivots let into the lower edge of the nameboard.

Right: Hauling a tandem axle bulk powder tanker with its own blower equipment, this 1973 T3448XB Borderer with Gardner '240' wears the proud livery of Sutton & Son, St Helens. The 240bhp 8LXB engine made its debut in 1970 and Atkinsons with this engine had a wider radiator grille to provide additional cooling.

Left: The practice of naming individual model types only got going from about 1970. The bulk of production was divided between Borderer 2-axled tractor units and Defender rigid eights. The six wheel 'Searcher' seen here in the livery of paper makers Chapman & Co. was a less common sight. VTD495M has a 6LX '150' and dates from 1974.

Right: Any traditionally liveried Atkinson takes some beating and lorries in the Rochdale-based J & T Sharrocks' fleet were particularly eye-catching. This 1974 Borderer artic was photographed on a beautiful sunny afternoon in 1979, being unloaded at the large British Industrial Plastics factory in Birmingham.

Left: H. Parkinson of Cleveleys, Blackpool, were big users of Atkinsons and this 1974 Gardner '240'-powered Borderer T3448XB coupled to a bulk powder tanker must have been the pride of the fleet. It was photographed when brand new and its appearance is considerably enhanced by Parkinson's striking livery.

Right: With a design gcw of 38 tons the 'Leader' was a rear-steer model announced in 1970. This version with a 6LXB '180' would have been rated at 32 tons. It was part of the Northern Ireland Trailers fleet from Preston. NIT was part of the Coast Lines Group which was absorbed into P&O. The tractor unit has been preserved since being retired.

Left: This smart T3446RR is a fine example of a mid-1970s Borderer from the famous Beresford fleet from Tunstall, Stoke-on-Trent. One of Beresford's leading customers was H & R Johnson, manufacturers of Crystal Tiles. The old established haulier sold out to Bassetts of Tittensor in 1997.

Right: Henleys Transport of Goudhurst, Kent was one of the few companies to run eight wheelers on general haulage in the 'seventies. This 30ton gvw Defender L3086XB with a 30ft flat dates from 1973. Henley's specialise in the transport of fresh produce and are now part of the WRM/Coolchain group.

Right: The Cummins 220 was the biggest rival to the Gardner '240'. The T3446C, like this one of the Bridgewater Transport Services division of the Manchester Ship Canal Company, was the popular choice of many fleets but they never quite matched up to the Gardner-powered jobs for durability and resale value.

BRIDGEWATER
BRIDGEWATER
TRANSPORT
SERVICES
MANCHESTER
ATKINSON
BORDERER
77
77
ANB 214 M

Left: Still gleaming with fresh paint, this virtually new 1973 T3046XB Borderer had just joined the Smiths of Bury fleet and was captured on film a long way from base at Kirkcaldy in Fife.

Right: British and proud of it - this 1974 Gardner '240'-powered Borderer T3448XB, coupled to a 40ft flat loaded with steel coils, came from the beautifully liveried Adam Jones fleet based at Blackheath in the heart of England.

75

Left: Wm. Dobson of Edinburgh opted for Rolls Royce power for their new T3446RR Borderer, DWS621L. Dobson's attractive livery sets the Mk.2 cab off well on this artic tank outfit engaged on European traffic. It was photographed when new at Scratchwood Services on the M1 just north of London. Dobson ran a large fleet of around ninety Atkinsons. In the 'sixties it included a rare four-cylinder Detroit Diesel powered L944GM tanker on contract to Esso.

Right: The Mk.2 cabbed 'Silver Knight' was hard to distinguish from a Borderer at first glance but this T3046XB just pre-dates the Borderer. Registered in 1970 it was part of the large William Nuttall fleet from Clifton, Manchester. Nuttall's were operating about 40 Atkinsons in the early 'seventies when they were absorbed into the Devon based Renwicks Freight Group.

Left: Just as the Mk.2 cabbed 'Silver Knight' was a Borderer look-alike, so the Defender could easily be mistaken for a late 'Black Knight' 26 ton gross rigid eight. This 1971 eight wheeled flat with demountable fridge van in the livery of D. Stevens of Wick doesn't carry a Defender badge but the changeover point from Black Knight to Defender is vague. ESX917J was powered by a Gardner 6LXB and almost certainly qualifies as a Defender.

Right: This early Borderer artic, like the Stevens eight wheeler, falls in that 'grey area' between the Mk.2 Silver Knight and the fully-fledged Borderer. Though powered by a '180' Gardner it was able to gross at 32 tons. It was part of the notable John Raymond fleet from Bridgend in South Wales - one of the finest Atkinson fleets in the area.

Left: Passing the old St Katherine's Dock bonded tea warehouses on the northern approach to London's Tower Bridge is a T3446XB bulk powder artic from the memorable fleet of W & J Riding, once based at Longridge, Preston. ETF510J dates from 1971 and was part of a 75-strong fleet. Riding's was part of the Transport Development Group.

Right: Posing outside the Burton's Biscuits factory in Blackpool, Lancs is this smart 180bhp T3046XB Borderer artic dating from 1971. It is coupled to a 40ft Crane-Fruehauf van advertising Burton's famous 'Wagon Wheels'.

Left: This 1970 TRS3266XB of Welch's Transport Ltd, Stapleford, Cambridge was just 18 months old when photographed on the A1301 at Great Shelford. It is powered by a 6LXB '180' Gardner.

Right: Defenders were available on a choice of two wheelbases. The shorter version was limited to 26 tons gvw. This 1974 bulk tipper of W.H. Phillips of Wirksworth is seen threading its was through the narrow main street of Ampthill in Bedfordshire in August 1978.

Left: A superb example of a Defender bulk tipper, one of a number operated by Bexton & Smith of Coalville near Leicester. The 1975 vehicle carries a 30 ton plate and its '180' Gardner gives exactly the required six bhp per ton. It has a 25cu.m Stevecastle tipping body for coal haulage.

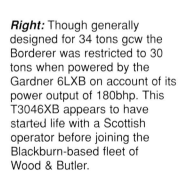

Right: Though generally designed for 34 tons gcw the Borderer was restricted to 30 tons when powered by the Gardner 6LXB on account of its power output of 180bhp. This T3046XB appears to have started life with a Scottish operator before joining the Blackburn-based fleet of Wood & Butler.

Above: Walkersteel of Grantham, Lincs were still operating this 1975 Borderer in 1986 when this shot was taken. The 11-year-old veteran had put in a lot of hard work but looked none the worse for it. Atkinson fibreglass cabs, if looked after, would soldier on indefinitely, the steel back panel being the only part likely to suffer corrosion.

Right: A long serving Gardner '240' powered Borderer from the famous Bassett Group of Tittensor, Stoke-on-Trent. It was about eleven years old when this shot was taken in 1986 and the trailer side-guards, required by law from 1983, are proof of its long service. GRF895N carries the fleet name 'Paula'.

Above: This Cummins-engined Borderer of Aidley's was another long haul veteran with about twelve years to its credit. Note the 'pigeon loft' sleeper - a feature often seen on latter day Borderers engaged on long distance work.

Part 4 : Something different

Left: Moves to modernise Atkinson's traditional image resulted in the striking 'View Line' cab, launched in 1966. This preceded the Mk.2 cab by some three years and, of the 200 or so built, nearly all were fitted with the dummy 'outside rad'. The original Viewline had a wide ornamental grille reminiscent of Leyland's Ergomatic but that wasn't accepted as it no longer had that much loved Atkinson character. View Line cabs were exclusive to tractor units including a number of heavy haulage 6x4s like this Cummins-engined Pickfords 55 ton outfit dating from 1971.

Right: This, the earliest example of a View Line, was new to R. Hall (Sidcup) Ltd and was originally used to haul timber out of Tilbury Docks. It soon passed to Factory Plant Removals of Handsworth, Birmingham in whose livery it appears here. This shot was taken in 1970.

Left: A 1969 Viewline artic operating in the fleet of J. Barrett of Delph near Oldham, seen hauling a latex tank within British Vita's Middleton factory in 1978. It is a Gardner '180' engined 'Silver Knight' T3246XB new to tissue paper manufacturers Robert Fletcher & Son of Greenfield.

Right: This 75 ton gcw T7566C Viewline of Wynns of Newport has the Mk.2 cab with the sturdy upper bumper characteristic of these purpose-built heavy haulage tractors. They were powered by a Cummins NTC-290 and featured a Kirkstall D80-13-2 rear bogie.

Left: Aimed chiefly at the export market, the 50 ton gtw BT1366 of the early 'sixties was available with a choice of Cummins and Rolls Royce engines from 212 to 335bhp. Kirkstall overhead worm rear axles were fitted. This work-worn example was used internally at a large steel works in Newport.

Right: One of Atkinson's numerous bids to modernise its image came in the form of the 'tin front' or 'Bodyline' Mk.1 cab which first appeared around 1963. It was fussy in appearance and cut little ice with Atkinson customers who were seemingly quite happy with the solid looking traditional style rad. When this 1965 S2486X tipper was new, one or two Atkinsons were still appearing with 'bow front' cabs and external cast aluminium radiators were still standard fitment.

Left: In anticipation of expansion into the European market, Atkinson set up an operation in Belgium but their fibreglass cab would not be marketable in Europe. Fried Krupp of Essen who had just pulled out of truck building agreed to supply their stylish steel tilt cab to Atkinson who grafted it on to their Silver Knight chassis. Very few were built so this British example is quite a rarity. All 'Atkinson-Krupp' tractors were Rolls Royce powered.

Right: Atkinson's Australian operations got under way during the 'sixties and a new breed of truck was developed for their 'home' market and New Zealand. This was quite different from UK-sourced Atkinsons and from 1966 a locally designed cab (nick-named the 'Skippy') was introduced. It was built by Rein-forced Plastics Pty. At least one UK operator, R. Hanson of Wakefield, had a 'Skippy' cabbed eight wheeler after one was featured at the 1968 Earls Court Show demonstration park. This New Zealand example was still at work in Hawkes Bay in 1993.

Left: Still hard at work after more than twenty years, this F-3870 stock truck was photographed in Fremantle, W.A. in February 2000. Australian Atkinsons were a breed apart with their Cummins or Detroit Diesels up to 450bhp and their unique design of fibreglass tilt cab.

Right: After Seddon Atkinson was formed in the UK in 1970 its Atkinson Australia subsidiary was sold off, becoming part of International Harvester Australia. When International Harvester withdrew from the market to reform as Navistar in 1984, ITAL (International Trucks Australia Ltd) became an independent operation and marketed a new breed of Atkinson featuring the T-line cab from their ACCO model. This example was seen operating in New Zealand in the early 'nineties. Since 1992 ITAL has been part of Iveco.

CLASSIC ATKINSONS 1

S.1586 Specification

ATKINSON 8 WHEEL 15 TON CHASSIS - MODEL S.1586

ENGINE. Is the Gardner 6LW. 6 cylinder compression ignition direct injection diesel unit, having 4½" bore 6" stroke, developing 112 h.p. at the governed speed of 1,700 r.p.m., and a torque of 358 lbs.ft. at 1,300 r.p.m. The massive seven bearing crankshaft is carried in a deep section rigid crankcase, the dry linered cylinders being arranged in twin blocks of three, with detachable heads and overhead valve location; pistons are fitted with chromium plated gas rings, all features ensuring long life with ease of maintenance. Forced lubrication to all crankshaft bearings is provided by submerged gear pump housed in the large capacity sump, with strainers on both suction and delivery circuits. Cool air manifolding is standard, and air cleaner can be fitted if required. Ample cooling is provided by the large diameter fan and centrifugal water pump, the system being thermostatically controlled. The particular feature of this unit is fuel economy ensured by the specially designed fuel pump, controlling by centrifugal governor the amount of fuel injected. Ready starting from cold by electric starter and positively driven dynamo are other features. The engine, as a unit, with clutch and gearbox, is three point mounted, with rubber insulation at each location.

CLUTCH. Is a 16" single dry plate type, provided with a clutch stop and ample two stage adjustment to cater for full liner wear. Clutch slip torque is 510 lbs. ft., more than equal to all calls from the driver, and yet smooth in operation under all conditions.

GEARBOX. Mounted as a unit with the engine. This unit has five forward speeds and reverse, top gear being direct, controlled by one change speed lever only. All gears are in high quality heat treated alloy steel, mounted on large diameter rigid shafts, carried on bearings of ample capacity. The ratios are selected to suit the arduous duties the chassis will perform, and are as follows:

Gear	Ratio	Road Speed	1,700 r.p.m.	Axle ratio 6fl
Fifth	1 : 1	29.10 m.p.h.		
Fourth	1.565 : 1	18.60 m.p.h.		
Third	2.74 : 1	10.60 m.p.h.	With 9.00-20 (12 ply) tyres	
Second	4.68 : 1	6.25 m.p.h.		
First	7.92 : 1	3.68 m.p.h.		
Reverse	7.92 : 1	3.68 m.p.h.		

TRANSMISSION. Power is transmitted to the driving axle by a single piece tubular propeller shaft. Shaft incorporates needle roller wide angle universal joints into sliding couplings. All shafts are dynamically balanced to eliminate vibration.

REAR AXLES. Drive to the road wheels is provided by twin overhead drive worm axles having 7¾" centres, coupled by a needle bearing universally jointed (wide angle) shaft. The foremost axle incorporates a third differential or torque divider, ensuring that each axle accepts an equal proportion of the driving torque, and eliminating tyre scrub. Axles are fully floating, the drop forged hubs being mounted on ample capacity taper roller bearings, in turn mounted on a solid one-piece forged axle casing. Alternatively single 8½" driving and trailing axle can be provided for this model for favourable conditions.

FRONT AXLES. The twin front axles are independently sprung, each having an I Section drop forged beam. The hubs also are drop forgings, mounted on taper roller bearings. King pins are mounted on roller bearings to provide easy steering, the ball jointed track rods being located at the rear of the axles. Braking is provided on the leading axle only, and is hydraulic foot operated.

SUSPENSION. Front - comprises long semi-elliptic silico manganese springs, shackled at the rear, to provide comfortable riding. **Rear** - is by four semi-elliptic silico manganese springs, fixed at their outer ends to take the driving torque, and coupled at their adjacent ends by a balance beam to form the bogie. This balance beam whilst equalising the load between the two driving axles, allows for varying road surfaces. Rocking motion of the balance beam due to road surface unevenness automatically lubricates all wearing surfaces of the suspension system, by means of a piston type oil pump, which is fed from and returns surplus oil to reservoir, thus minimising maintenance of this unit. All shackle pins are of case hardened alloy steel.

FRAME. Frame side members are of high tensile steel pressings 11" x 3" x 1" braced by substantial pressed steel crossmembers fitted with high tensile bolts. Front and/or rear drawbars can be fitted as an extra, with hand and/or power operated trailer brake equipment.

RADIATOR. Is of the detachable " Still " tube type, with separate top and bottom tanks of ample water capacity. Temperature control is by thermostat, allowing quick warm-up under cold conditions. Oil cooling can be fitted as an extra for overseas.

STEERING. The steering is of the " Marles " type totally enclosed, working in oil, and of the double roller/cam design, to give easy operation with minimum backlash throughout its range of operation. Both front axles are interconnected by a twin drag link arrangement, the geometry being so arranged to provide the accurate lock angles required in this form of construction, eliminating uneven tyre wear.

BRAKING SYSTEM. The footbrake acts on all wheels and is hydraulic servo assisted. Drums on all wheels are 17" diameter, the front shoes being 3" wide, the rear 6" wide, both being internal expanding. The ratchet type handbrake, located to the right hand, acts on the rear wheels only, and is mechanically operated throughout.

ROAD WHEELS AND TYRES. Pressed steel disc wheels are carried on the hubs by ten 0.875" diameter wheel studs, tyres being 9.00-20 (12 ply) single front and twin rear.

FUEL TANK. Is of 30 gallons capacity mounted on the nearside of the chassis frame. Feed is by Amal pump, camshaft driven, and consumption approximates under normal conditions to 10-11 m.p.g.

ELECTRICAL EQUIPMENT. Is 12 volt double pole system, with battery of ample capacity; instruments housed in panel in front of driver; head, side and tail lamps are provided, controlled by dipper switch. Electric starting is standard.

CHASSIS EQUIPMENT. Includes speedometer, electric horn, hydraulic jack, front and rear number plates, grease gun, complete set of tools and wheel stud covers; lubrication chart, service manual and spare parts lists are provided with each chassis.

LEADING DIMENSIONS (ft. ins).

Wheelbase	15'	1½"
Rear Bogie centres	4'	4¼"
Overall length of chassis	22'	10¼"
Overall width of chassis	7'	5¾"
Back of cab to end of frame	17'	10¼"
Frame height (laden)	3'	1¼"
Ground clearance (laden)		10"
Frame width	3'	2"
Front wheel track at c/line	6'	4¼"
Rear wheel track	5'	7"
Turning circle	60'	0"

EXPORT FEATURES.

Engine. Air cleaner is standard.
Rear Axles. For arduous duty overseas, the worm centres are 8½", with the ratio adapted to suit the conditions required; the third differential is eliminated, positive drive for sandy conditions thus being assured.
Radiator. Tropical type with integral oil cooling can be provided for extreme temperature conditions.
Braking System. Air pressure braking can be supplied to all braked wheels, the compressor being engine driven. Tyre inflation is fitted as standard, and trailer lines can be supplied.
Steering. Right or left hand steering and controls can be provided.
Tyres. Single and twin 11.00-20 (12 ply) or 10.00-20 (12 ply) low pressure tyres are fitted for all overseas models.

EXTRAS The following special fittings can be supplied at extra charge.

(a) Gear box driven power take-off.
(b) Trailer brake hand and/or power operated.
(c) Spring loaded trailer drawbar (either laminated or coil).
(d) Front tow bar.
(e) 8½" centre single driving and trailing axles can be provided.

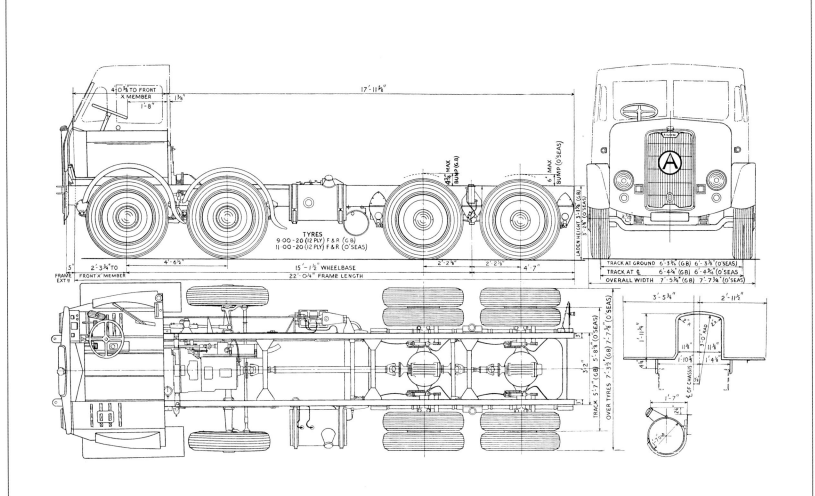

GENERAL ARRANGEMENT DRAWING
ATKINSON S.1586 CHASSIS
(early 50's)

Approximately 1:50 scale

CLASSIC ATKINSONS 2
TS.1065 / TS.1066 Specification

ATKINSON 6-WHEELED CHASSIS - MODELS TS.1065 & TS.1066 - 16 TON GROSS VEHICLE WEIGHT

ENGINE. Is the Gardner LW compression ignition direct injection diesel unit, having 4¼" bore, 6" stroke, and is either of the following units in this range :-

Model	Engine Type	No. of Cylinders	H.P. at 1700 R.P.M.	lbs,/ft. Torque at 1300 R.P.M,	No. of main Bearings
T.S.1065	5LW	5	94	300	6
T.S.1066	6LW	6	112	358	7

In all the above models the crankshaft is carried in a deep section rigid crankcase, the dry linered cylinders being arranged in twin blocks, with detachable heads and overhead valve location; pistons are fitted with chromium plated gas rings, all features ensuring long life with ease of maintenance. Forced lubrication to all crankshaft bearings is provided by submerged gear pump housed in the large capacity sump, with strainers on both suction and delivery circuits. Cool air manifolding is standard, and air cleaner can be fitted if required. Ample cooling is provided by the large diameter fan and centrifugal water pump, the system being thermostatically controlled. The particular feature of this unit is fuel economy ensured by the specially designed fuel pump, controlling by centrifugal governor the amount of fuel injected. Ready starting from cold by electric starter and positively driven dynamo are other features. The engine as a unit, with clutch and gearbox, is three point mounted, with rubber insulation at each location.

CLUTCH. Is a 16" single dry plate type, provided with a clutch stop and ample two stage adjustment to cater for full liner wear. Clutch slip torque is 510 lbs./ft., more than equal to all calls from the driver, and yet smooth in operation under all conditions.

GEARBOX. Mounted as a unit with the engine. This unit has five forward speeds and reverse, top gear being direct, controlled by one change speed lever only. All gears are in high quality heat-treated alloy steel, mounted on large diameter rigid shafts, carried on bearings of ample capacity. The ratios are particularly selected to suit the arduous duties the chassis will perform, and are as follows:

Axle & Ratio		WORM 6¾	WORM 6¼
Tyres		9.00-20(12 ply)	9.00-20(12 ply)
Engine R.P.M		1700	1700
Gear	Ratio	Road Speeds	M.P.H.
Fifth	1 : 1	29.10	31.40
Fourth	1.565 : 1	18.50	20.00
Third	2.74 : 1	10.60	11.50
Second	4.68 : 1	6.20	6.70
First	7.92 : 1	3.66	3.96
Reverse	7.92 : 1	3.66	3.96

TRANSMISSION. Power is transmitted to the driving axle by two-piece tubular propeller shafts, incorporating needle roller bearing wide angle universal joints, and sliding coupling to allow full axle articulation. Supported at the centre by a self-aligning ball race. All shafts are dynamically balanced to eliminate vibration.

REAR AXLE. Drive to the road wheels is provided by an overhead drive worm axle, having in the case of 5LW engine model, 7¾" centres fitted with a standard ratio of 6¾ with the following alternative ratios available to suit the conditions required, i.e,, 6.25, 7.25 and 8.25 to 1. For the 6LW engine model an 8½" centre heavy duty axle is fitted with a standard ratio of 6¼ with the following alternative ratios available 6.75, 7.25 and 8.25 to 1. The axle is fully floating, the drop forged hubs being mounted on ample capacity taper roller bearings, in turn mounted on a solid one-piece forged steel axle casing.

FRONT AXLE. The twin front axles are independently sprung, each having a one-piece I section high tensile steel beam of generous proportions, the forged steel hubs mounted on taper roller bearings. The king pins are mounted on taper roller bearings to provide easy steering; the ball jointed adjustable track rod being mounted at the rear,

ROAD SPRINGS. Front and rear are semi-elliptic, silico manganese steel, of suitable length, shackled at the rear, to ensure smooth riding under all conditions.

BRAKING SYSTEM. The footbrake acts on all wheels and is hydraulic servo assisted. Drums on all wheels are 17" diameter, the front shoes being 3" wide, and the rear 6" wide, all being internal expanding. The ratchet type handbrake, located to the right hand, acts on the rearmost front and rear axle wheels only, and is mechanically operated throughout,

ROAD WHEELS AND TYRES. Pressed steel disc wheels are carried on the hubs by ten 0.875" diameter wheel studs, tyres being 9.00-20 (12 ply) or alternatively C-20 Michelin metallic, single front and twin rear.

STEERING. Is the Marles Cam and double roller type, totally enclosed and working in oil. All contacting surfaces are of hardened alloy steel, wear being minimised and development of backlash practically eliminated. Both front axles are interconnected by a twin drag link arrangement, the geometry being so arranged to provide the accurate lock angles required in this form of construction, eliminating uneven tyre wear. Can be supplied with either right or left hand steering and controls.

FRAME. Frame side members are of high tensile steel pressings 10.875" x 3" x 0.32" braced by substantial pressed steel cross members fitted with high tensile bolts,

RADIATOR. Is of the detachable "Still" or "Withnell" tube type, with separate top and bottom tanks of ample water capacity. Temperature control is by thermostat, allowing quick warm-up under cold conditions.

FUEL TANK. Is of 32 gallon capacity mounted on the nearside of the chassis frame. Feed is by Amal pump mounted on and driven by the engine.

ELECTRICAL EQUIPMENT. Is 12 volt (24 volt alternative with 6LW model) double pole system, with batteries of ample capacity; instruments housed in panel in front of driver. Twin head, side and stop/tail lamps are provided, head lamps controlled by dipper switch. Electric starting is standard.

CHASSIS EQUIPMENT. Includes speedometer, electric horn, hydraulic jack, loose starting handle, rear number plates, grease gun, complete set of tools and wheel stud covers; lubrication chart, wiring diagram, service manual and spare parts lists are provided with each chassis.

EXTRAS.
- (a) Coil or leaf spring rear lowing jaw.
- (b) Front lowing member.
- (c) Front bumper bar (chromium).
- (d) Trailer brake, hand and/or power operated.
- (e) Air pressure brakes.
- (f) Power take-off (gear box driven).

EXPORT FEATURES.

Engine. Air cleaner is standard.

Road Wheels and Tyres. 10.00-20 (12 ply) or Michelin metallic tyres of equivalent rated capacity, single front and twin rear are fitted for all overseas models.

Steering. Right or left hand steering and controls can be provided.

Radiator. Tropical type can be supplied for extreme temperature conditions, (with integral oil cooler on 6LW engine model only.)

Extras. Coach-built drivers cab.
All steel drivers cab.
Overspeed gearbox in lieu of direct.

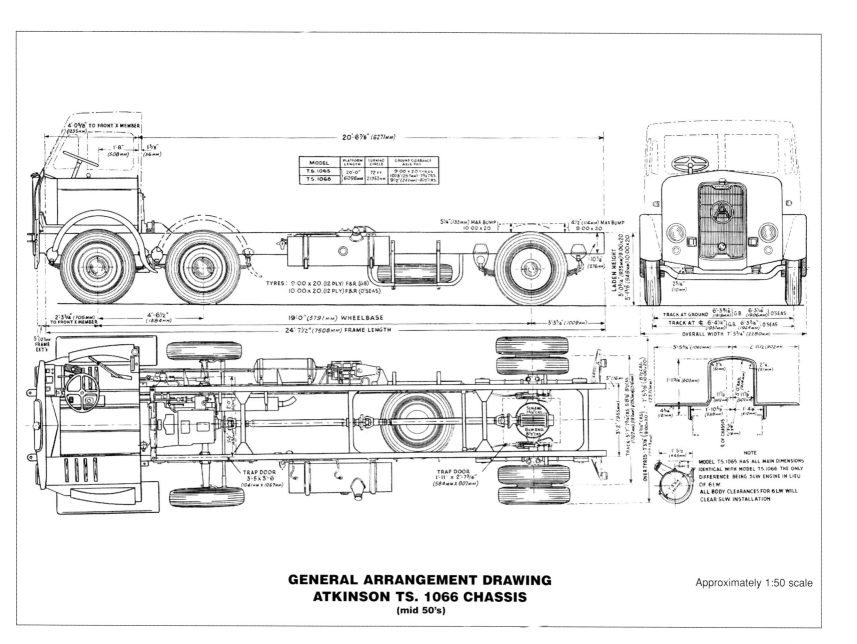

GENERAL ARRANGEMENT DRAWING
ATKINSON TS. 1066 CHASSIS
(mid 50's)

Approximately 1:50 scale

CLASSIC ATKINSONS 3
TS. 3266C Specification

ATKINSON 6 WHEELED TWIN-STEER TRACTOR CHASSIS MODEL TS. 3266C. FOR 32 TON G.V.W.

ENGINE. The Cummins NH 220 diesel engine is fitted in this range and has the following features:-
No. of Cylinders 6
H.P. at 2100 R.P.M. 212
Torque at 1300 R.P.M. 585 lb./ft.
KGM Torque at 1300 R.P.M. 80.9

Bore (ins.) 5¼"		Bore (mms.)	130.175
Stroke (ins.) 6"		Stroke (mms.)	152.4
Capacity (cu. ins.) 743		Capacity (litres)	12.17
Compression Ratio 15.5 : 1			
Water Capacity (Galls.) 5.8		Water Capacity (litres)	22.7
Oil Capacity (Galls.) 5.83		Oil Capacity (litres)	26.4

CLUTCH. This is an 18" diameter (547.2 mm.) single dry plate type provided with a clutch stop and ample adjustment to cater for full liner wear. Lining area for this clutch is 310 sq.ins. (2000 sq. cms).

GEARBOX. The standard gearbox in this 32 ton gross range is the Z.F. AK6-75 six-speed overdrive.
Gear ratio details are as follows:

Gear	Ratio
6th	0.72 : 1
5th	1.00 : 1
4th	1.62 : 1
3rd	2.61 : 1
2nd	4.10 : 1
1st	6.44 : 1
Reverse	5.92 : 1

TRANSMISSION. Power is transmitted to the rear axle by a single tubular propeller shaft, i.e., Hardy Spicer 1700 series. Needle roller bearing wide angle universal joints with sliding coupling gear are incorporated. All shafts are dynamically balanced to eliminate vibration.

REAR AXLE. The type of axle in this range of vehicle is the Kirkstall 8″ double helical axle. This is a double reduction type of axle, the primary reduction being obtained by spiral bevel gears and the secondary reduction by double helical gears. The standard ratio is 7.01 : 1 but the following ratios are available : 5.2 : 1, 5.78 : 1, 6.28 : 1, 7.95 : 1 and 9.17 : 1.

FRONT AXLES. The twin front axles are of the I section high tensile beam type with forged steel hubs mounted on taper roller bearings and have 65.08 mm. stub axles.

ROAD SPRINGS. Springs on the front axle bogie are semi elliptic of silico-manganese steel shackled at the rear. The standard front springs are 3½" wide (88.9 mm.) and have 48" crs. (flat) (1219.2 mm). The rear springs are 3½" wide (88.9 mm.) and have 54½" crs. (flat) (1384.3 mm).

BRAKING SYSTEM. An air pressure actuated footbrake operates on all axles through diaphragm type wheel cylinders. The drum diameter and widths being 16"x5" on the front steering axles and 15"x7" on the rear axle. A ratchet type handbrake located to the driver's offside acts on the second steering front axle and the driving axle and is mechanically operated throughout.

ROAD WHEELS & TYRES. Pressed steel disc wheels are mounted on the hubs by ten 0.875in. dia. wheel studs.
Standard tyre equipment being:
Front axle bogie: 9.00x20 Michelin 'X' or 9.00x20 14-ply mounted on B7.0x20 6" offset (152.4mm.) wheels.
Rear axle: Michelin D.20X or 10.00x20 16-ply mounted on B7.0x20 6" offset (152.4 mm.) wheels.

STEERING. Is the Marles cam and roller type totally enclosed and working in oil. Self-adjusting ball sockets are fitted to the track rod, drag link, drop arm and top steering lever. Steering wheel 21" diameter (533.4 mm).

FRAME. Frame sidemembers are high tensile steel pressings 10.875" X 3" x ¼" (276.2 mm. x 76.2 mm. x 7.94 mm.) and braced by pressed steel crossmembers fitted with high tensile fitted bolts.

RADIATOR. The engine is fitted with a non-pressurised detachable 90-tube radiator. Temperature control is by a "bellows' type thermostat. Frontal area of radiator is 4.58 sq.ft. (0.425 sq.mtr). Capacity of radiator is 5.45 gallons (24.775 litres).

FUEL TANK. Tank capacity is 45 imperial gallons (204.6 litres) mounted on the nearside of the chassis. An electric fuel gauge is fitted on the instrument panel in the cab.

ELECTRICAL EQUIPMENT. 24 volt lighting and starting is fitted as standard and is an insulated return system incorporating a 30 amp alternator; twin head, side, stop and tail lamps are fitted as standard.

CAB. This is the timber framed cab with fibreglass panels, the timber being best quality Ash, having excellent all round visibility. All controls and instruments are within easy reach of the driver. Both driver's and mate's seats are fully adjustable. A padded bonnet cover is fitted as standard, as are wing mirrors, heater and twin demisters, flashing indicators, chrome front bumper and twin headlamps.

CHASSIS EQUIPMENT.   Includes the following :-

Hydraulic jack & handle	Lubrication chart	Grease gun	Wiring diagram
Complete set of tools	Service manual	Wheel Hub covers	Spare parts list

EXTRAS AVAILABLE.

Cab:-	Chassis:-
Illuminated sign panel in cab roof	Full Torque P.T.O. and controls.
Plain cab roof	Front push bar
Sheet rack and facia board	Full width towing and bumper bar
"Hit and Miss" dash ventilators	Aeon rubber suspension
Single rotary flashing beacon	Shock absorbers
Fog, spot, loading and reversing lamps	Steering gear lock
60 Amp alternator	Engine hand throttle control
Air washers and Air wipers	Wheel step rings
Air horns	
Chapman "Superide" seat	
Water temperature gauge and Ammeter	
Oil pressure warning device	
Tachometer	
Speedograph time and distance recorder	
Hubometer (mileage recorder)	
Varivane automatic shutters	
Radiator muff	

Vehicles built to Petroleum Regulations will have the following features:-

Firescreen at rear of cab	Special fibreglass panels	Fireproof glazing rubber
Battery master switch	made with fireproof resin	Front crosswise silencer

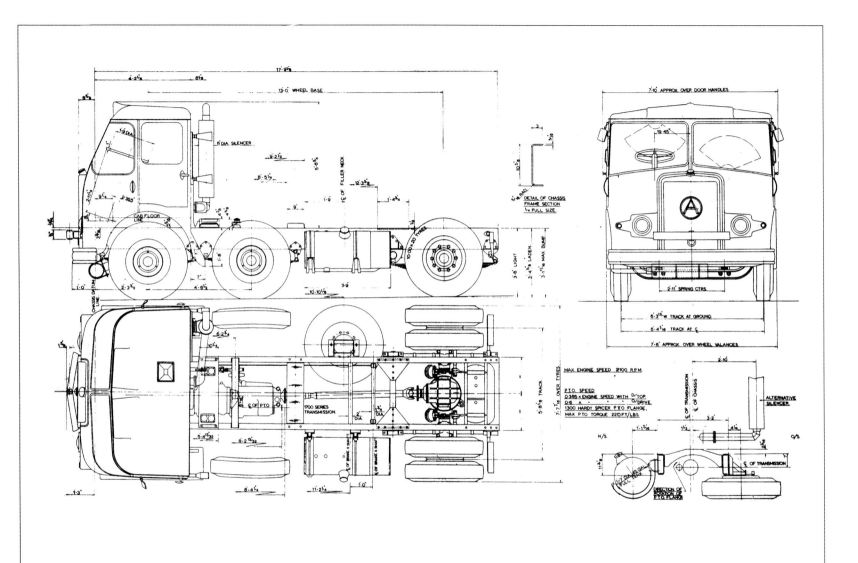

**GENERAL ARRANGEMENT DRAWING
ATKINSON TS. 3266C CHASSIS
(mid 60's)**

Approximately 1:50 scale

CLASSIC ATKINSONS 4
T. 3046C Specification

ATKINSON 4 WHEELED TRACTOR CHASSIS for 30 TON GROSS VEHICLE WEIGHT

There are three Models in this range, all are powered by Cummins engines. Models available are as follows :-

MODEL	Engine	Gearbox	Rear Axle
T. 3046C	Cummins NHE180	Z.F. AK6-75	Kirkstall 8¼" D/Helical Rear Axle
T. 3046C	Cummins NH220	Z.F. AK6-75	Kirkstall 8¼" D/Helical Rear Axle
T. 3046(L)C	Cummins NH220	Z.F. AK6-75	Kirkstall 8¼" D/Helical Rear Axle

ENGINE   **Cummins NHE180.** No. of Cylinders 6

Bore 5¼" (130.175 mms.)	lb/ft Torque at 1100 R.P.M. 520
Stroke 6" (152.4 mms.)	KGM Torque at 1100 R.P.M. 71.9
Capacity 743 cu. ins. (12.17 litres)	Water Capacity 5.83 gals. (26.4 litres)
Compression Ratio 15.6 : 1	Oil Capacity 5.83 gals. (26.4 litres)
H.P. at 1950 R.P.M. 173	Approx. Weight 5360 lbs. (1073 kgs.)

ENGINE   **Cummins NH220.** No. of Cylinders 6

Bore 5¼" (130.175 mms.)	lb/ft Torque at 1300 R.P.M. 585
Stroke 6" (152.4 mms.)	KGM Torque at 1300 R.P.M. 80.9
Capacity 743 cu. ins. (12.17 litres)	Water Capacity 5.00 gals. (22.7 litres)
Compression Ratio 15.5 : 1	Oil Capacity 5.83 gals. (26.4 litres)
H.P. at 2100 R.P.M. 212	Approx. Weight 2360 lbs. (1073 kgs.)

CLUTCH. This is an 18" diameter (457.2 mm.) single dry plate type provided with a clutch stop and ample adjustment to cater for full liner wear. Lining area for this clutch is 310 sq ins. (2000 sq. cms).

GEARBOX. The standard gearbox in this 30 ton gross range is the Z.F.AK6-75 6-speed overdrive. Details of the gearbox are as follows:

6th.	0.72 : 1	2nd.	4.10 : 1
5th.	1.00 : 1	1st	6.44 : 1
4th.	1.62 : 1	Reverse	5.92 : 1
3rd.	2.61 : 1		

TRANSMISSION. Power is transmitted to the rear axle by a single tubular propeller shaft i.e., Hardy Spicer 1700 series. Needle roller bearing wide angle universal joints with a sliding coupling are incorporated. All shafts are dynamically balanced to eliminate vibration.

REAR AXLE. The type of axle in this range of vehicle is the Kirkstall 8¼" double helical axle. This is a double reduction type of axle, the primary reduction being obtained by spiral bevel gears and the secondary reduction by double helical gears. Standard ratio is 7.01 : 1. but the following ratios are available : 5.2 : 1, 5.78 : 1, 6.28 : 1, 7.95 : 1 and 9.17 : 1.

FRONT AXLE. This is a one-piece H section high tensile beam with forged steel hubs mounted on taper roller bearings and has 65.08 mm. dia stub axles.

ROAD SPRINGS. Both front and rear are semi-elliptic, of silico-manganese steel shackled at the rear. The standard front springs are 3½" wide (88.9mm.) and have 48" crs. (flat) (1219.2 mm). The rear springs are 3½" wide (88.9 mm.) and have 54" crs. (flat) (1384.3 mm).

BRAKING SYSTEM. An air pressure actuating foot brake operates on all axles through diaphragm type wheel cylinders, The drum diameter and widths being 16"x5" on the front axle and 15"x7" on the rear axles. A ratchet type hand brake located to the driver's offside acts on the rear wheels only and is mechanically operated throughout. When a definite decision has been reached by the Ministry of Transport, a supplementary leaflet describing the system will be issued.

ROAD WHEELS & TYRES. Pressed steel disc wheels are mounted on the hubs by ten 0.875" diameter wheel studs. Standard tyre equipment being Michelin D20'X' or 10.00x20 16-ply mounted on B7.00x20 6" offset (152.4mm).

STEERING. Is the Marles cam and roller type, totally enclosed and working in oil. Self-adjusting ball sockets are fitted to the track rod, drag link, drop arm and top steering lever. Steering wheel 21" diameter (533.4 mm).

FRAME. Frame sidemembers are high tensile steel pressings 9"x3"x⅜" (234.9 mm. x 76.2 mm. x 9.53 mm) and braced by three pressed steel cross-members fitted with high tensile fitted bolts.

RADIATOR. The engine is fitted with a non-pressurised detachable 90-tube radiator. Temperature control is by bellows type thermostat. Frontal area of radiator is 4.58 sq. ft. (.0425 sq.mtr). Capacity of radiator is 5.45 imperial gallons (24.775 litres).

FUEL TANK. Tank capacity 54 imperial gallons (245.5 litres) mounted on the nearside of chassis. Feed to the engine is by the Amal pump mounted on and driven by the engine. Electric fuel gauge is fitted on the instrument panel in the cab.

ELECTRICAL EQUIPMENT. 24 volt lighting and starting is fitted as standard and is an insulated return system incorporating a 30 amp alternator; twin head, side, stop and tail lamps are fitted as standard.

CAB. This is the timber framed cab with fibreglass panels the timber being best quality Ash, having excellent all round visibility. All controls and instruments are within easy reach of the driver. Both driver's and mate's seats are fully adjustable. A padded bonnet cover is fitted as standard, as are wing mirrors, heater and twin demisters, flashing indicators, chrome front bumper and twin headlamps.

CHASSIS EQUIPMENT includes the following :-

Hydraulic jack & handle	Lubrication chart	Grease gun	Wiring diagram
Complete set of tools	Service manual	Wheel hub covers	Spare parts list

EXTRAS AVAILABLE ON REQUEST.

Cab :-	Chassis :-
Illuminated sign panel in cab roof	10 H.P. David Brown P/T.O. and controls
Plain cab roof	Sheet rack and facia board
"Hit and Miss" dash ventilators	Martin Harper P/T.O. and controls
Single rotary flashing beacon	Full Torque P.T.O. controls
Fog, spot, loading and reversing lamps	Front push bar
60 amp alternator, Tachometer	Full width towing and bumper bar
Air washers, Air wipers and Air horns	Cary's laminaire rear suspension
Chapman "Superide" seat	Aeon rubber suspension
Water temperature gauge & Ammeter	Shock absorbers
Oil pressure warning device	Hand control for trailer brakes
Speedograph time & distance recorder	Engine hand throttle control
Hubometer (Mileage recorder)	Steering gear lock
Varivane automatic shutters	Wheel step rings
Radiator muff	

Vehicles built to Petroleum regulations will have the following features:-

Firescreen at rear of cab	Special fibreglass panels	Fireproof glazing rubber
Battery master switch	made with fireproof resin	Front crosswise silencer

106

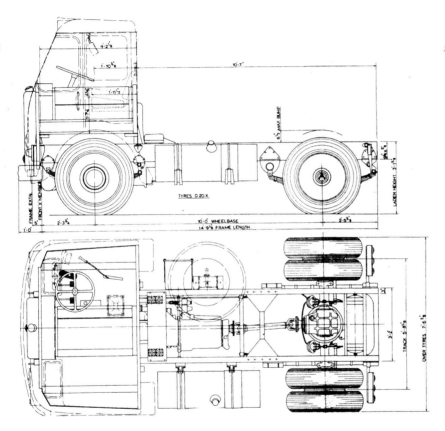
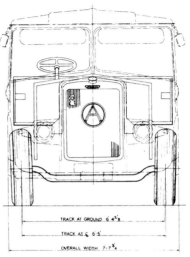

GENERAL ARRANGEMENT DRAWING
ATKINSON T. 3046C CHASSIS
(mid 60's)

Approximately 1:50 scale

CLASSIC ATKINSONS 5
'Borderer' Tractor Specifications

MODEL.	Engine.	Specification.
T. 3246XBL	Gardner 6LXB	Displacement 638 cu ins Max bhp 180 @ 1850 rpm Max torque lbs ft 536 @ 1050 rpm
T. 3446C	Cummins NHK-220	Displacement 743 cu ins Max bhp 215 @ 2100 rpm Max torque lbs ft 590 @ 1550 rpm
T. 3446C	Cummins NHK-240	Displacement 855 cu ins Max bhp 240 @ 2100 rpm Max torque lbs ft 660 @ 1500 rpm
T. 3448XB	Gardner 8LXB	Displacement 851 cu ins Max bhp 240 @ 1850 rpm Max torque lbs ft 696 @ 1050 rpm

Kysor or Varivane radiator shutters are an option on Cummins-engined models.

CLUTCH. The Borg and Beck 17AS steel-strap-drive clutch is used behind the Gardner 6LXB dieseL it is a 17ins diameter single dry plate type with a total friction area of 320 sq ins.

The Lipe-Rollway 14-2PT clutch is used behind the Cummins 220 and 240 and Gardner 8LXB engines and is a spring-loaded, two-dry-plate, pull type clutch with a friction area of 423 sq ins.

GEARBOX. The six-speed David Brown 06-600 overdrive gearbox is fitted on the T3246XBL tractor Ratios are 1st 6.61, 2nd 3.91, 3rd 2.45, 4th 1.56, 5th 1.00, 6th 0.72, reverse 5.76.

For the three more powerful tractors, two gearboxes have been selected from the British-built Fuller Roadranger series. The 10-speed Roadranger RTO-610 gearbox is used with the Borderer with the Cummins NHK-220 diesel and has ratios of 1st 7.25, 2nd 5.66, 3rd 4.42, 4th 3.43, 5th 2.77, 6th 2.11, 7th 1.56, 8th 1.29, 9th 1.00, 10th 0.805, reverse 7.66 and 2.23.

The 9-speed Roadranger RTO-9509A gearbox is used with the other tractors and has ratios of 1st 8.77, 2nd 5.85, 3rd 4.29, 4th 3.2, 5th 2.37, 6th 1.83, 7th 1.34, 8th 1.00, 9th 0.74, reverse 9.17 and 2.86.
A variety of power take-offs are available for all three types.

FRONT AXLE. One piece H section beam, forged and heat treated. Drop forged stub axles, swivels mounted on parallel king pins. Plain bushes top and bottom, roller bearing thrust race. Hubs mounted on adjustable taper roller bearings.

REAR AXLE. All four models feature the advanced Seddon Atkinson SA-13-HR hub reduction driving axle with cam brakes. The hub gearing provides a 4:1 reduction which greatly reduces the torque loadings on the half shafts and the spiral bevel gears have an extra large pinion, normally the weakest point of an axle.

Optional is the Kirkstall D85-10-2 axle, which is also a double reduction design, with secondary reduction in the hubs. The three Borderers with 6-cylinder engines can also have Eaton axles-the two-speed 19800 type on the T.3246XBL and the single-speed 9800 on the two T.3446C's.

RATIOS.

SA.13.HR	5.47	6.12		
D85-10-2	5.04	5.605	6.118	6.823
9800	5.60	6.63		
19800	4.87/6.63			

SUSPENSION. High-deflection 56 ins semi-elliptic leaf springs are used at the front, with the axle placed forward of the centres to improve ride and give better braking action.
Semi-elliptic springs are used at the rear, being 53.5 ins long (loaded).

BRAKE SYSTEM. The pipe layout is one of the neatest on any European truck, aiding both brake efficiency & fault-finding. The Borderers have a triple line air pressure operated system with dual diaphragm type lock actuators, size 24 on the front axle and size 30 on the rear.
The footbrake pedal controls two main systems through a dual footbrake valve, the split circuits controlling tractor and trailer braking separately but simultaneously. There is an auxiliary, hand-controlled system controlling the tractor front axle brakes and trailer brake and a parking brake operating on the tractor axles.
A load-sensing device is fitted on the rear axle which regulates and balances braking effort automatically in relation to the load being imposed on that axle.

WHEELS AND TYRES. One-piece drop-centre wheels, size 7-50 x 22.5 6ins offset, mounted by ten 0.875 ins dia studs. Spare wheel and tyre in winch-type carrier. Standard tyres are tubeless 11-22.5.

FRAME. Sidemembers and crossmembers are manufactured from high tensile steel pressings. Sidemembers are 10.875 x 3 x 0.3125 ins section and the crossmembers are joined to them by fitted bolts and nuts. Fuel tank capacity is 62 imp galls.

CAB. The Mark 2 driver's cab is the result of 15 years experience by Atkinson with glassfibre-reinforced plastics. Repairs are easily carried out at a fraction of the cost of repairing or replacing steel and each cab is hand made by craftsmen.

A powerful 6-9 kW fresh-air heater with booster fan is installed within easy reach of the driver and has outlets near floor level for driver and mate and through five vents below the windscreen. An independent fresh-air ventilation system has its ram intakes high on the front of the cab, just below the windscreen, and feeds through two interior 'Spherivent' multidirectional or complete shut-off controls. The driver sits within easy reach of all controls and switches and in great comfort on a Chapman Superide seat with full hydraulic suspension.
Cab options include construction to Petroleum Regulations and roof platform.

ELECTRICAL. 24 volt insulated return system incorporating 30 amp CAV AC524 alternator. Two 12 volt batteries in series.

INSTRUMENTS. Mounted in front of driver on black non-reflecting fascia panel. Speedometer with distance recorder, tachometer, three air pressure gauges, fuel gauge, water temperature gauge, oil pressure gauge and battery condition indicator.

SERVICE AIDS. Supplied as standard are a spare wheel and carrier, complete set of tools, hydraulic jack and handle, lock actuator release connector, grease gun and service publications.

ESTIMATED KERB WEIGHTS*

	Front Axle			Rear Axle			Total		
	T	C	Q	T	C	Q	T	C	Q
T. 3246XBL	3	7	0	2	7	2	5	14	0
T. 3446C/220	3	9	1	2	7	2	5	16	3
T. 3446C/240	3	13	2	2	7	2	6	1	0
T. 3448XB	3	13	0	2	8	0	6	1	0

* Weight of chassis and cab complete with 5th wheel, oil, fuel, water, tools, spare wheel and tyre.

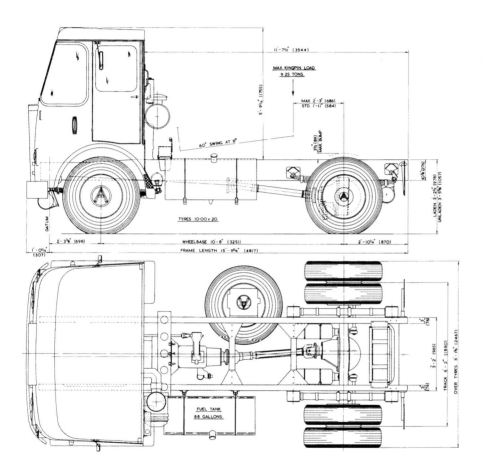

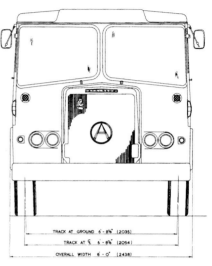

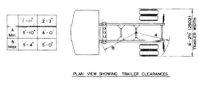

PLAN VIEW SHOWING TRAILER CLEARANCES.

MILLIMETRES SHOWN IN BRACKETS.

**GENERAL ARRANGEMENT DRAWING
ATKINSON 'BORDERER' T. 3446C CHASSIS**
(early 70's)

Approximately 1:50 scale

109

CLASSIC ATKINSONS 6
'Leader' Tractor Specifications

MODEL.	Wheelbase	Engine	Design Gross Weight	Plated Gross Weight
TRS. 3666C	11ft 6ins.	Cummins NHK-230	36 tons	32 tons
TRS. 3866C	11ft 6ins.	Cummins NHK-230	38 tons	32 tons
TRS. 3868XB	11ft 6ins.	Gardner 8LXB	38 tons	32 tons
TRS. 3868XB	12ft 6ins.	Gardner 8LXB	38 tons	32 tons

ENGINE.	Gardner 8LXB	
	Displacement	851 cu ins
	Max bhp	240 at 1850 rpm
	Max torque (lbs ft)	696 at 1050 rpm
	Cummins NHK-230	
	Displacement	855 cu ins
	Max bhp	230 at 2100 rpm
	Max torque (lbs ft)	620 at 1500 rpm

CLUTCH. A Borg and Beck 18R4 heavy-duty clutch is used on the Cummins-powered model designed for 36 tons. It is an 18ins diameter single dry-plate type with a total friction area of 310 sq ins.
The other three Leader tractors have the Lipe-Rollway 14-2PT clutch. This is a spring-loaded, two-dry-plate, pull type clutch with a friction area of 423 sq ins.

GEARBOX. The ZF AK6-75 constant mesh gearbox is used on the 36-ton model in the Leader range. Engagement is by dog clutches and it has ratios of: 1st 6:44, 2nd 4:1, 3rd 2:61, 4th 1:62, 5th 1:0, 6th 0:72, reverse 5:92.

For the heavier 38-ton Leader tractors, the gearbox is a British-built Fuller Roadranger RTO-909A unit. The 9-speed Roadranger RTO-909A has ratios of: 1st 8:77, 2nd 5:85, 3rd 4:29, 4th 3:2, 5th 2:37, 6th 1:83, 7th 1:34, 8th 1:00, 9th 0:74, reverse 9:17 and 2:86.

A variety of power take-offs are available.

FRONT AND SECOND AXLES. Reversed Elliott I beam types of generous proportion with 2.56ins stub axles and a capacity of 14,000 lbs each. Forged steel hubs are mounted on taper roller bearings.

REAR AXLE. Two differing makes and types of driving axle are fitted on the Leaders. One is the new Kirkstall D85-10-2, which is a double reduction design with secondary reduction in the hubs and a pressed steel casing. It features a lockable differential which is air operated. The other driving axle is the Eaton 9800, a double reduction unit with spiral bevel and planetary gear.

The Kirkstall axle is the standard fitment on the 38-tonners with the Gardner 8LXB diesel. while the Eaton axle is standard on the 36-tonner. Either axle can be used on the 38-tonner with the Cummins power unit.

SUSPENSION. High-deflection 56ins semi-elliptic leaf springs are used at the front, with the axle placed forward of the centres to improve ride and give better braking action. Semi-elliptic springs are used at the rear, being 53.5ins long (loaded) when used with either axle.

The second steering axle is located longitudinally by quarter-elliptical springs acting as trailing links. A double shackle arrangement provides the lateral location behind the axles on the 38-tonners.
A Panhard rod arrangement is used on the 36-tonner Air bellows between the springs and the frame carry the load and air can be released to increase the weight on the driving axle for increased adhesion

BRAKE SYSTEM. The pipe layout is one of the neatest on any European truck, aiding both brake efficiency and fault-finding. The Leaders have a triple line air pressure operated system with dual diaphragm type lock actuators, size 24 on the front axle and size 30 on the driving axle. Size 12 single diaphragms are used on the second steering axle.

The footbrake pedal controls two main systems through a dual footbrake valve, the split circuits controlling tractor and trailer braking separately but simultaneously. There is an auxiliary hand-controlled system controlling the tractor front and driving axle brakes and trailer brakes and a parking brake operating on the front and driving axles.

A load-sensing device is fitted on the rear axle which regulates and balances braking effort automatically imposed in relation to the load being imposed on the second and driving axles. A Jacobs engine brake is available with the Cummins engine.

WHEELS AND TYRES. One-piece drop centre wheels, size 7.50x22.5 6ins offset, mounted by ten 0.875ins dia studs. Standard tyres are tubeless 11-22.5.

FRAME. The side-members are produced from steel pressings with a 23 tons per sq ins yield and crossmembers are carefully positioned to give controlled flexibility. The crossmembers pick up the webs of the chassis sidemembers and span almost the full depth of the chassis frame. The frame side is 10.875ins deep, with a 3ins wide flange and 0.3125ins thick section.

Two 34 gallon fuel tanks are a standard fitment.

CAB. The Mark 2 driver's cab is the result of 14 years working experience by Atkinson with glassfibre-reinforced plastics. Repairs are easily carried out at a fraction of the cost of repairing or replacing steel and each cab is hand-made by craftsmen.

A powerful 6.9kW fresh-air heater with booster fan is installed within easy reach of the driver and has outlets near floor level for driver and mate and through five vents below the windscreen. An independent fresh-air ventilation system has its ram intakes high on the front of the cab, just below the windscreen, and feeds through two interior 'Spherivent' multi-directional or complete shut-off controls.
The driver sits in a relatively high position within easy reach of all controls and switches in great comfort on a Chapman Superide seat with full hydraulic suspension,

Cab options include construction to Petroleum Regulations and roof platform.

STEERING. ZF column power steering gear is used, providing quick response and effortless handling. On the 36-tonner type 7425 is used, while the heavier type 7429 model is fitted on the 38-tonners.

INSTRUMENTS The instruments are grouped together in front of the driver. The panel is easily detachable for maintenance. It contains separate air pressure gauges for the three brake systems, electrically-driven speedometer and tachometer, fuel gauge, water temperature gauge, battery condition indicator and oil pressure gauge. There are warning lights for alternator, trailer direction indicator and reversing lamp (if fitted).

There is a warning buzzer for low air pressure and warning bell for differential lock (if fitted).

ELECTRICAL SYSTEM. 24 volt insulated return system incorporating 30 amp CAV alternator. Two 12 volt batteries in series and CAV 3L5 starter motor.

SERVICE AIDS. Supplied as standard are a 6-ton hydraulic jack and handle, complete set of tools, grease gun and service publications.

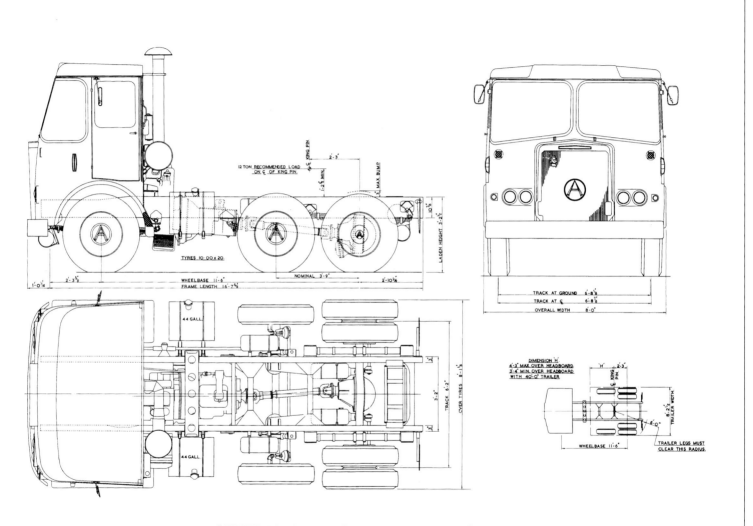

GENERAL ARRANGEMENT DRAWING
ATKINSON 'LEADER' TRS. 3868XB CHASSIS
(early 70's)

Approximately 1:50 scale

SUMMARY OF LEADING ATKINSONS THROUGH THE YEARS

STEAM
1916-1929: 4T, 5T, 5T/T, 6T

DIESEL
'Flat-front' cab 1934-1952

1934-1935: '3-4 TON', '6-7 TON', 'R6 10-12 TON'
1935-1936: FC43 & FC47 (4w), FC56 (6w)
1936-1937: FCG46 & FCG57 (4w), FCG56 & FCG57 (6w)
1937-1940: S/M/L644, S/M/L744, S/M/L745 (4w),
S/M/L1165 (6w), S1486 & M1586 (8w)
1937-1942: M/L965 (Twin-steer 6w), L1065, S/M/L1265 (6w)
1937-1952: L1586 (8w)
1945-1952: L644, S/L744, L745 (4w), T746 (4w tractor),
S/M1266 (6w)
1950-1952: T1266 (HD export tractor)
1951-1952: S644, S745, L745L, S746, L746L (4w),
T1268 (HD export tractor), S1586 (8w)

'Bow-front' cab 1952-1964

1952-1953: S644, L744, S/L745, L745L (4w)
1952-1956: S/M/L/T1266, M/T1268 (6w), S/L1586 (8w)
1952-1964: L644, S/L/T746, L746L (4w)
1953-1956: L1588 (8w)
1954-1955: L746EXL (4w)
1955-1964: TS1065, TS1066 (Twin-steer 6w)
1956-1959: L1788 (8w)
1956-1964: ST1044 (4w tractor, auto coupling), S/L946,
L946EXL (4w), S/M/L1366 (6w), S/L1786 (8w)
1959-1964: ST1045 (4w tractor, auto coupling)
1961-1964: L645, T744, T745, M746, S/L945 (4w)
1961-1962: TS965 & TS966 (Twin-steer 6w)
1961-1964: S2086 (Export HD 8w)

Mk.1 Fibreglass Cab 1958-1968

1958-1964: L644, S/L746, T746, L746L, S/L946,
L946EXL (4w), S/M/L1366 (6w),TS1065,
TS1066 (Twin-steer 6w),S/L1786 (8w)
1959-1964: ST1045 (4w tractor, auto coupling)
1961-1962: TS965, TS966 (Twin-steer 6w)
1961-1964: L645, T744, T745, M746, S/L945 (4w),
S2086 (HD export 8w)
1963-1964: 'Weightmaster'
WS/WM/WL45, WL45L (4w),

Mk.1 Fibreglass Cab 1958-1968 (continued)
WT45 (4w tractor), WM/WL65T (6w),
WL86T (8w)
1964-1966: M/L1645E, M/L1646E, L1645LE,
L1646LE (4w), M/L2266 (6w), S/L2486 (8w),
ST1845E (4w tractor, auto coupling), T2446,
T2646, T2846, T3046 (4w tractors),
T3266 (6w tractor)
1966-1968: 'Gold Knight' - S1645E, S1646, S2066,
S2266, S2486
'Black Knight' - L1645, L1646, M2266,
L2486, L2686
'Silver Knight' - T2245, T2246, T2846,
T3046, T3246, T3266

Mk.2 Fibreglass Cab 1968-1975

1968-1971: 'Gold Knight' - S2066, S2266, S2486, S2686
'Black Knight' - M/L2266, L2486, L2686
'Silver Knight' - T3046, T3246, TRS3266,
T3866, T4566
1970-1972: 'Raider' L1646, 'Leader' TRS3666, TRS3866,
TRS3868
1970-1975: 'Searcher' S/L2466, 'Defender' S/L3086,
'Borderer' T3446, T3448, T3046
1972-1974: 'Venturer' T4566, T4568, T7566, T7568

OTHER MODELS

'Body Line' 1963-c.1966
A modernised full-fronted version of the Mk.1
fibreglass cab was available on most models.

'View Line' 1966-1970
The 'View Line' cab was available on 'Silver
Knight' tractor units as an alternative to the
Mk.1 and Mk.2 cabs.

Semi-bonneted tractors 1963-1964
'Semi-bonneted' SBT3246X and SBT3266X
tractor units, built mainly for Pickfords.

Bonneted tractors 1961-1966
BT1366X and BT1366C (BT3266C from 1965)
tractors for 40-50 ton gtw. The 90 ton gtw
Omega was built 1957-64.

Other Models (continued)
Half-cab dumpers 1958-1966
DT745 and DT746 (4w) were available from
1958-65. DT1366 and DT1866 (6w) were
available 1958-66.

'Guardsman' 1964
The T3048C 'Guardsman' was a semi-
experimental 4w tractor with 'FE' (Forward
Entry) cab and Cummins V8E-235 engine.

Atkinson-Krupp 1969-1970
Some 'Silver Knight' tractors (CLT3846RR)
and 'Black Knight' 6x4 rigids were built with
Krupp tilt cabs, mainly for the European
market.

'Supa Cab' six wheelers c.1972
Heavy duty 6x4 export models with Seddon
cab. S2666C (tipper), L2666C (truck) and
T4566C (tractor).

Gritters 1958-1964
Special 6x6, and some 8x6, gritter and
snowplough chassis built for the Ministry of
Transport.

Overseas Models
As well as the above U.K. sourced models
there were numerous Atkinson types built at
overseas plants including Australia and South
Africa to suit local operational conditions.

Note:
While every effort has been made to ensure accuracy, this model list
is, by necessity, simplified and is meant to give a broad indication of
the Atkinson range. Certain suffixes indicating engines and braking
systems have been omitted and dates are approximate.